Jari's Year

by Louise Franklin

NATIONAL
GEOGRAPHIC
LEARNING

CENGAGE

Meet Jari. He is from Lagos, Nigeria.
Now he lives in Houston, Texas.

Houston is the fourth largest city in the United States.

It is Jari's first year in the United States.
What will he do this year?

Lagos is the largest city in Nigeria.

In January, Jari goes to his new school.
He learns to speak English.

This is Jari's high school in Houston.

Mrs. Ortiz is Jari's English teacher.
She thinks he speaks English very well.

**February 21 is Jari's sixteenth birthday!
Now he can learn to drive a car.**

Jari takes lessons
at a driving school.

Mr. Lang is Jari's driving teacher.
He teaches Jari to be a safe driver.

Jari goes to a school dance in March. The dance is called the Turnabout Dance. Girls ask boys to go to the dance.

Everyone has a good time at the dance.

Jari's friend Oni asks him to the dance. She likes Jari a lot.

In April, Jari gets a job at the grocery store. He works after school on Tuesdays and Thursdays.

Jari stocks produce at the store.

Mr. Reynolds is his boss. He thinks Jari is a hard worker.

During the last week of May, Jari takes his final exams. He passes them all!

Jari gets an A on his algebra exam.

$$\left(x + \frac{b}{2a}\right)^2 = \frac{b^2 - \ }{\ }$$

$$x + \frac{b}{2a} = \pm \frac{\sqrt{b^2 - 4a}}{2a}$$

$$x = \frac{-b \pm \sqrt{b}}{2}$$

(A)

Nice Work!

Ms. Lee is Jari's algebra teacher. She is proud of Jari.

In June, Jari plays sports at the park.
He makes some new friends.

Jari is really good at soccer.

Marco is Jari's new friend. He wants
Jari to join the school soccer team.

In July, Jari and his father go to a baseball game. They watch the Houston Astros play the Washington Nationals.

The Astros win!

Jari catches a foul ball!

Jari tries out for the school soccer team in August. He makes it!

At the tryouts, the boys have to move fast.

Mr. Ruiz is the soccer coach.
He makes the team practice hard.

Poor Jari! He has bad luck at his first soccer game in September. He trips and sprains his ankle.

Jari has to go to the hospital.

EMERGENCY

AMBULANCE

Dr. Martinez looks at Jari's ankle.
She wraps it in a bandage.

OCTOBER

In October, Jari goes to the homecoming football game. The football team plays against its biggest rival.

The game is very exciting.

Jari watches Oni cheer. He likes her a lot!

Hooray for Jari! He passes his driving test in November. Now he can drive a car by himself.

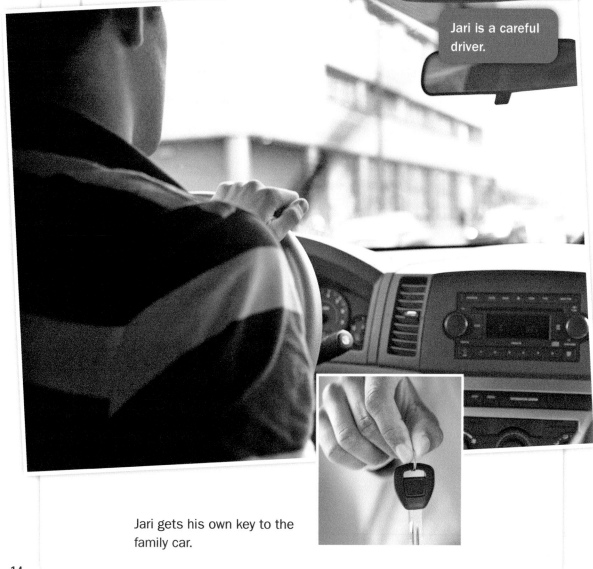

Jari is a careful driver.

Jari gets his own key to the family car.

On December 31, Jari and his family celebrate New Year's Eve. They also celebrate their first year in the United States.

Jari and his family go out for dinner at their favorite restaurant in Houston.

Outside, fireworks light up the Houston sky. Happy New Year!

Later, Jari thinks about everything he did.
What an exciting year!